(perishable)

(perishable)

Lisa Kirschke

RESOURCE *Publications* · Eugene, Oregon

PERISHABLE

Wipf & Stock
An Imprint of Wipf and Stock Publishers
199 W. 8th Ave., Suite 3
Eugene, OR 97401

www.wipfandstock.com

PAPERBACK ISBN: 978-1-6667-3057-9
HARDCOVER ISBN: 978-1-6667-2226-0
EBOOK ISBN: 978-1-6667-2227-71

Cover art & print layout by: Greg Kirschke

To mom

Margaret Ann Pearson

"I will likely not even try"

•

Most miracle
is in
impossible
to talk about
orchestration
seam ripped
reweave
sou fiber
unseen

The eternal
conversation
is terribly,
quiet.

It also
brings

unreasonable
comfort.

●

Sometimes
I have // to stop //
thanking you
because

. . . I
can t
say
thank you
enough

And so I wonder (slash)
ask,

"Is t understood?"

(because I have other
things
I could be doing...)

And the beautiful thing
is:
It so completely is:

I start
thanking you,
again.

●

God wrapped in flesh
do you suffer, yet?

linear line
giving finite mind
... narrative

intersects with:
up/down descent
outside of time

holding up
this body

maybe it still shows up
as light
this impossible crossing

when you are with me
it is in all ways
including this:

•

¡angry baby!

I demard to be lifted out

of here !

NOT...carried through...

The scenery is horrible.

It's. Been.Years.

"untitled seventeen"

Do you feel
the empty air
as you
twitch obsess
throw arm
sling yourself
into the next
entice and temporary
intimate fix
of dying
anyway?

Meanwhile,
more and more
snail writhe
twist of
future hooks
and fists
beginning as
abandon
(it tricks!)
wrap, wrap, wrap
themselves into
counterfeit
currencies?

This is not freedom.

Sometimes,
sweet and thick
swamp filled lungs
scream "More!"
and
receive,
recline,
receive,
every
damned
thing

Till they collapse

strung out still
from their
poison pour

It's just too sticky
and the lightness is
missing.

(Do you know what I mean?)

or

Maybe
you
generate

-illusion-
transfix
and stop
All the ask
reflect
... pull
down shades
and re-set
(yourself inside
        self
     -void
         inside)
       self

This works.
(as a hover pause)

holding spot
(temporarily)

until seedlight
continues call
and
final confront

grows

from that
very quiet
where you've
just completely trusted
everything
I've
just
said
in the last
ten breaths

because
somehow
you KnEw
it came
from Love

This.

This is real
suffer bliss
This is where

(Jesus is.)

35

Take a piece
Take a drink

open fear eternal

•

We are

chalk seashell
frail

... and

dried
-bird yellow -
Bones

distinct (5!)
flights,

and we think

we rule

some kind
of
some kind
of

universe.

"city eye avoidance"

I want taste.

men-al flavored

aluminum

in formless grape-of

no consequence

crepe-creep sweet

and crispy thin

solid in question

layers between

wrat is

and isn't

sin.

"backwᴐrds spelled"

shopkeep-jestor-king
your scepter-
glasswhiskey
still waves wild high
and your
spit-fly
spirit
still sticks
expertly
as mock laughter
slaughters
angel hair
birdecaged
in a rising pitch

but your eyes,
they never fly.
and you don't
(much) court agape's
entrance in

How will you feed
your next hungry ghost
when the yeast breast
rise of dying men,
is never enough bread?

"You're right; it can't be
proven or seen.

I'm muttering, unthinking,
                insane to believe."

but
... yet,
except
this)
I love this
unproven
I feel myself
being loved
day always
in cloudscape
soft movement

canopy cover
sheer
prism layer
pour

watercolor
choreography
plumb, harvest
thin gold
bright of pure
love flow
into glass
reflected light
and keeps
pouring
pours

pouring on
soak forest
rain
pouring on
drunken skin
thunder room
floors.

my cells
raise up
their cups
clink, wink
their
connections
and sing
while, after,
and before
drinking
because
prayer
becomes
thinking
and praise
becomes
breathing
in this,
sovereign
abundance

"I don't make that many
                    promises anymore."

the moment before
you accept
into your being
... of belief
actually
accept
that story
revealing
the heart
the narrative
of the god man
taking all of it in
eating everything
that separates us
from him

it is like
looking over the edge
of carved cavern wide
where
sharp rock
climbs atop
sharp rock
reaching
with their teeth

to
gnaw/saw/sand
beautiful blue high

your eyes open width
breathing in
eminent

you exhale
body leans
foot stutters

Wait.

Who throws themselves
off the mountain side?

I promise
you are caught
and cradled
inside
love's
interior

even with
your angry fists
infinite conversation
begins

Yes, you will be talking
crazy
but really, who cares?
for the many reasons
of the world

When there is
forever this?

"One day, I'll fall in
forever, but I won't drown.
I'll learn different
breathing."

You are streaming
my window
doesn't argue
everywhere
filtered through
shifting centers
You tease out relational
spectrum relationships

I am tasting
plumb bridal gown
transparency
living inside
of each
sweet water
circle round
bite

You end as
sour sharp
shape note
swallowed
down
at some
point
(undefined)
becoming
me

You are always bringing.

(Sometimes it's
lifted from
my cell awareness
and knitted with soft air
to carry me
through the day

You offer winter diffused
five-forty-five
Houston neighborhood

Is that your peace
courting
the twilight?
She says, "Yes, all right,
I'll stay..."

You are always bringing.

You turn up
forest volume vision
watch the soft moss
green
lift its own golden aura

It is cheering you!
from a quiet sun spot
somewhere
in Alaska)

such true
soft spoken
need not
always be
amplified
!!
just welcomed
like movement
between

My words
disappear
My edges diffuse
My being pieces
fade -disseminate-
as they reach

but without
their former fear

I have no
more monument
need...

for when this body
- scrapped clean -
is gnawed and
sanded back
again
texture soft
between fingers

soft with
rot's sovereignty

Your ants will not be
overwhelmed
by the sweetness
celebration

They will simply
colonize
around a feast
of
survival
and
survival
lost
While I...

I will be

Swimming

●

my heart is growing back
:
living colored crystal